PRIMERS
Volume Three

PRIMERS
Volume Three

Romalyn Ante

Aviva Dautch

Sarala Estruch

Selected by Hannah Lowe
and Jane Commane

Nine
Arches
Press

Primers: Volume Three
Romalyn Ante, Aviva Dautch, Sarala Estruch
Selecting Editors: Hannah Lowe and Jane Commane

ISBN: 978-1-911027-40-9

Cover artwork / Primers logo © 3Men^2
www.3men.co.uk

First published April 2018 by:

Nine Arches Press
Unit 14, Sir Frank Whittle Business Centre
Great Central Way, Rugby
CV21 3XH
United Kingdom

www.ninearchespress.com

Printed in the United Kingdom by:
Imprint Digital Ltd.

Nine Arches Press is supported using public funding by Arts Council England.

Supported using public funding by
**ARTS COUNCIL
ENGLAND**

Primers

Volume Three

is produced in partnerhip with:

About the Selecting Editors

Hannah Lowe's first poetry collection *Chick* (Bloodaxe, 2013) won the Michael Murphy Memorial Award for Best First Collection and was shortlisted for the Forward, Aldeburgh and Seamus Heaney Best First Collection Prizes. In September 2014, she was named as one of 20 Next Generation poets. She has also published three chapbooks: *The Hitcher* (Rialto 2012); *R x* (sine wave peak 2013); and *Ormonde* (Hercules Editions 2014). Her family memoir *Long Time, No See* was published by Periscope in July 2015 and featured as Radio 4's Book of the Week. Her second collection, *Chan,* is published by Bloodaxe. (2016). She is the current poet in residence at Keats House

Jane Commane is a poet, editor and publisher. Her first full-length collection, *Assembly Lines,* was published by Bloodaxe in 2018. In 2016, she was chosen to join Writing West Midlands' Room 204 writer development programme. A graduate of the Warwick Writing Programme, for a decade she also worked in museums and archives. Jane is editor at Nine Arches Press, co-editor of *Under the Radar* magazine, and is co-author, with Jo Bell, of *How to Be a Poet,* a creative writing handbook (Nine Arches Press). In 2017 she was awarded a Jerwood Compton Poetry Fellowship.

CONTENTS

Sarala Estruch

INTRODUCTION

Primers is a mentoring and publication scheme developed and run by the Poetry School and Nine Arches Press, which seeks to find, nurture and develop exceptional new poets.

The programme – now in its third year, and looking forward to a fourth – is a perfect example of what the Poetry School aims to do in all its activities: to encourage poets and poetry to flourish. With the support of Arts Council England, the Poetry School provides inspiring tuition at their teaching centres and online, from beginners' courses right through to an accredited MA with Newcastle University, as well as a wide range of opportunities for poets, including the Poetry in Aldeburgh Festival, and the Ginkgo ecopoetry prize.

But what unites all these strands is our aim to inspire poets, get them in front of an audience, and develop their careers. And that is exactly what Primers does. Each selected poet receives mentoring from a successful writer, this year from the brilliant Hannah Lowe, with editorial support from Jerwood Compton Poetry Fellow Jane Commane, and publication with Nine Arches Press, as well as a series of launches and festival readings to promote their work.

To find the perfect poets for *Primers: Volume Three,* the Poetry School, Jane Commane, and guest editor and mentor Hannah Lowe read through hundreds of submissions – each of which was a distillation of the hard work, love and craft of its author – searching for manuscripts that showed outstanding promise. Above all, we were looking for writers on the cusp of something – writers who, with a bit of guidance and support, could become vital and exciting new voices in contemporary poetry. And we're happy to say that we found them in Romalyn Ante, Aviva Dautch and Sarala Estruch.

The three poets in this year's Primers collection are writers of an exceptionally high quality, drawn from a pool of exceptionally high quality writing. What made these three poets stand out was the sense that they were at the right place for the kind of mentoring and editing that Primers offers, and that the manuscripts they submitted all had a clear and compelling arc and theme. This isn't necessarily a requirement of the Primers selection, but in these cases, it did stand out.

Aviva Dautch's poems are characterised by a beautiful fluency and precision of image. The subject matter of many of them is a mother and daughter relationship affected by the emotional disorder of hoarding. Thus, the poems are 'hoards' themselves, of words, objects and images, but what struck us about them is the way in which the poems provide order in the face of such chaos. We felt this possibility at work in the exquisite poems of Sarala Estruch as well – how poetry can help structure and perhaps process complex emotional material, in Sarala's case, the possibilities and challenges of cross-cultural relationships, both as a legacy of parents and in the current moment. Romalyn Ante's work also deals with cross-cultural dynamics – the experiences of a Filipino nurse in Wolverhampton – with a careful and nuanced approach to how language communicates these crossings and differences, and also with a persuasive sense of wonder.

What is remarkable about the work of all three poets, and what further stood out to us as readers, judges and editors, is their instinctive and distinctive *feel* for the way language can contain or capture these complex emotions and experiences. Interwoven here, within these crisp and lively poems, are common threads of homesickness, loss and distress – strong sensations that could so easily overpower a poem, yet are always handled by each poet with exacting attention and concision.

There is also each poet's tactility for the full possibilities of languages; dualities and multiplicities of languages, running in parallel not as separate entities within and alongside English. Tagalog, Japanese, Hebrew, Yiddish and Punjabi coexist, rub shoulders, slip across time and continents and form a part of the dialogue with the reader. And within this duality, the reminder that these poems are not about demarcations but commonalities; that language(s) carry the freight, but it is the poem itself which will open a dialogue with readers, in the heart and in the mind. A heart, after all, may be broken in Uttar Pradesh, hoarded with memories and history in a parent's house clearance in Salford, or beat its last heartbeat in a Wolverhampton hospital ward. As Sarala Estruch herself writes in her poem 'Consequences of Not Knowing My Father Tongue': "love carries more weight / than the human tongue".

The process of judging, editing and mentoring poets in Primers is an exciting and intense one, taking place over a compressed period of just six months from entries to the scheme closing, to the final poems being delivered and the book compiled and printed. Our hope in now presenting these three poets together is that you may take heart in their 'masterpieces' – with no hyperbole intended: the *Collins English Dictionary* defines the seventeenth-century origin of 'masterpiece' as coming from Dutch (*meesterstuk*) and German (*Meisterstück*) – and meaning "a sample of work submitted to a guild by a craftsman in order to qualify for the rank of master". Let us return to the origin of this word, and welcome these three talented poets of *Primers Volume Three* and their luminous, masterful poems which speak with hearts and tongues and demonstrate the full gravity of their craft. The future of poetry is in capable, skilled hands.

April 2018
Ali Lewis, the Poetry School
Hannah Lowe, Selecting Editor
Jane Commane, Nine Arches Press

Romalyn Ante

Romalyn Ante grew up in the Philippines and moved to the UK in 2005. She is a Jerwood/Arvon mentee (2017-2018). She is joint-winner of the Manchester Poetry Prize and received Creative Future Literary Awards for Poetry. She has also been Commended in the Battered Moons Poetry Competition. She has been featured in the *Vogue* article, '9 Poets to Know for World Poetry Day', and has been named by *FourHubs Magazine* as one of '10 Poets Bound to Shift UK Poetry.' She will be going back to the Philippines in 2018 as a Silliman University National Writers Workshop fellow to hone her craft. She is working towards her first full collection.

Half-empty

'The Philippines must be half-empty; you're all here running the NHS'
– Prince Philip, Duke of Edinburgh

Drug:
Migrationazoline (available in full or half-empty bottles)

Indications:
- prophylaxis of parents who nag like masonry drills, saying they did not send you to college to be a health-centre volunteer
- ulcers on the lips for eating kamote and kangkong every night
- chronic aching for a house and a garden of your own
- chest tightness and/or dyspnoea as you watch your child drool over Special Shaomai
- episodic blindness, secondary power-cuts

Contraindications:
- do not take this medicine if you have a weak heart or sensitivity to the tug of your child at your skirt

Cautions:
- your husband may look for another lover while you're gone
- your child may forget your name
- you may not be able to fly back home in time for your mother's burial

Side effects:
- drowsiness/vertigo/nausea
- behaviour changes (depends on how lazy your colleague is)
- weight loss (as you deprive yourself, ceaselessly converting pounds to peso)

- low mood (on occasions like Nochebuena)
- severe acne (unknown relatives who unexpectedly
  appear and demand money)
- bloating (as you yearn for the sweetness of lanzones or
  see flakes of desiccated coconut in the black November sky)
- intermittent euphoria (when you hand the bald girl
  her crocheted unicorn and her mother the Discharge Form)
- acute insomnia (when a kid on a stretcher is rushed
  through the door – his face blood-soaked, and for a second
  you think he's the child you left back home)

Anosmia

At first, it is uncomfortable,
and you must distract yourself,
burrow your nose through the half-
opened foil-lid of a Fortisip, or gaze
on the sky in the square window.

Soon, you get used to it: routinely part
your legs for the nurse with the lovely
skin, whose look you can never read:
has she got used to the scent of faeces
and urine? Is she just pretending?

You learn about anosmia, and kindness.
You stop saying 'Sorry, how embarrassing'.
You learn the weight of her touch,
the way a wipe glides down your groin.
The slight push of her palm on your hip.

You roll onto your side, and don't fear
falling off. You memorise the stories
of her get-aways, the cow ride, the man
who put a plumeria behind her ear,
her breath warming the end of your spine.

Way back home

The way home is a thousand leagues – Yi Yang-yon

This is the most important secret
my father told me:
Whenever you are lost,
you must turn your shirt inside out.

> As a family, we inverted
> our tropical-print vests
> when instead of white sands
> we found a barren land
> of black stones,
> wrecked plastic bottles
> like a smack of jellyfish.

I did it again with my blouse;
in childhood, when my siblings
left me by the rice-sack swing,
and my heart became a ripe makopa
with ants instead of seeds at the core.

> I followed my father's advice,
> and survived the hypnotic gaze
> of a pavo, and the buffalo
> standing as a gatekeeper
> between me and my path home.

Soon, I found the landmark:
the chapel
where my father confessed
his feelings for my mother, where
scents of sampaguita emanated
from Christ's stigmata.

Now, in a foreign land,
all the red buses are stranded.
I stroll in ankle-deep snow
back to the piss-scented flat
where my parents discuss
the divorce papers.

I stop under the lamp-lit flurry,
almost take my coat off
and turn it inside out.

Sayang

Tagalog: waste/ what a pity/ regret

There are things I regret.
I measure the distance of a star
with one stroke of breath.

*

In Malaysian and Indonesian
the word means 'Dear'
or 'to love'.

*

Sayang. If I hadn't left
I wouldn't be here,
peeling gauze from a wound.

*

At tea time, a woman flings
her plate of shepherd's pie
across the room.

Mince beef on the wall.
Sayang.
I wonder if there's more to life

than spit on my collar,
picking up Malteser-spheres
of faeces from the bed,

powdered drugs that fill
the cracks in my fingers.
Everyone says,

Don't leave.
Sayang ang benefits.
Sayang ang karma.

*

They say the brightest star
in the Philippine sky
is the same star in the UK.

*

Sometimes I lock myself
in the treatment room, tears
bloom on the hem of my skirt.

Sayang.
But I've got things to do
so I discard

all my *Sayang*
like used needles
into the yellow bin.

The Making of a Smuggler

after Zilka Joseph

It is never 30 kilos. Wherever we travel,
we pack the whole country with us.

We have our rice terraces as folded garments.
We plant pillars of trees – a rainforest

on a hairbrush. We dig bright orange crabs
out of white sands and use them as tabs

to zip our bags. We immigrants
are experts in packing. It's in our genes.

We know how to fill the landing card
but we're always ready for *No English.*

If the officer stops us, we let the smell
of old socks swirl up to his face like bats.

We'll let him dive into our belongings
like a man trying to fish in an ocean

ruled by sharp corals, stinging anemones.
He can squeeze the yellow packet harder

and not know it is pig's blood. He won't
hear the squeal as he chucks it aside;

he wasn't there, mud-soaked in a pen,
with the boy trying to catch an erratic swine.

The officer may ask, *No sauce?*
No chicken feet? in a Chinese accent

as if it would be easier for us to understand,
but he can't sniff my hand, see the sediments

in my nails: fermented fish and all
we dip in it. He can't cup his ear

with my palm, and discover the waves
of the Pacific. He can't follow me

through the gate – even with his gaze.
He'll miss the gleam of a red quill

in my lug sole, like when he didn't hear
my uncle's knife back and forth on a whetstone,

the way he slit the neck of my rooster, King Arthur,
giving me tips on how to cook for survival.

The officer did not feel the pot
of hot water getting lighter

when I poured it over the carcass.
He wasn't there, at that moment –

that perfect pause
before I plucked out all the feathers I used to stroke.

Antiemetic for Homesickness

A day will come when you won't miss
the country *na nagluwal sayo.*
You'll walk on gritted streets, light snow
will shawl you like a protective mother.

A vertigo of distant lights will not deceive you.
You may bury all the kisses of yesterday
in the fold of your handkerchief, the illuminated
star-shaped lanterns, the tansan tambourines.

But keep the afternoon your father sold his buffalo
to rent a jeepney to take you to the airport, keep
the driver who spat out phlegm, with the same
trajectory of a grasshopper landing on the ground.

Keep the list you wrote the night before you left,
promise you won't return till you become *someone.*
Keep the cassette tapes – your children's voices
shrill as the edges of winter stars.

Keep the booklet of *Our Lady of Perpetual Help*
in your uniform pocket, powder-blue
like her robe. Say the rosary,
feel each kamagong bead.

Rest on a pillow where you can hear the waves
of your lover's heart. Listen to Tagalog songs.
They will help you sleep through
the cold scratches of December.

Here's the tea-stained smile of a kababayan,
inviting you to a party. Go no matter how heavy
the day has been, and how many corpses
you have carried within.

Enjoy the home-cooked pansit,
the roasted pig's head, the blood-red apple
in its mouth. A day will come
when you won't need an antiemetic

for homesickness. You will accept,
wholeheartedly, the patient who always buzzes
for a commode, the search for the missing boot
of an A&E *habitué* – the village's drunk.

You will learn to heal
the wounds of their lives,
and the wounds of yours. Love, even the smoke
of a Black Country accent on your face.

So here's the karaoke mic –
sing your soul out till there's El Niño
in your throat, and you can drink
all the rain of Wolverhampton.

Learning Nihongo

(The Japanese occupied the Philippines from 1942-1945)

Kokoro – that's Japanese for heart,
hon for book, hana for flowers.
Ramen, her favourite noodle soup.
There's a guitar being plucked
from a one-bedroom apartment.
My grandmother asks,
Is that a bird on the balcony?
Kakashi is for scarecrow.

Komorebi is sunlight through the trees.
She waited for him until dusk
until the moon glowed, a yellow
antique plate. When the shootings
and the lootings subsided, he came.
She says, *Itadakimasu is what you say*
before stuffing food into your mouth.

Kintsukuroi. *Everyone should know*
what it means by now.
She did not care about gold rings,
she just wanted a hut in the field.
Yume is dream. Yuki is snow.
Don't confuse the two.

Her brain calcifies
and sometimes she forgets my name.
Wasuremono are forgotten things,
lost amidst the memorabilia
in a shoe box, and the sepia pictures
of herself as a provincial girl,
and him – an army man.

She says, hisashiburi is for long time no see
(though she's never used the phrase in her life).
It's for letting that one person smile at you
and depart like a gust of leaves.
It's for letting that one angle of his face
drown the darkness of a cave,
until you learn the word irusu –
until you learn to pretend you're not home
when he comes banging on your door.

Check-mate

i.
My father said, *Take advantage*
of the position of your pieces.

Do you think a crab-spider
camouflages itself on a petal
just to fit in?

Check-mate in four moves.

ii.
Suppose my life in the UK
is not unplanned, and this time

God is giving me the upper hand.
I pacify the cries of an old woman
for her long-cremated mother

with Lorazepam in a spoonful of yogurt.

iii.
No move is unplanned.
We walk together, palm-to-palm,

down *John Speelman Street* corridor.
We sit on a waiting bench,
a plastic robin perched
on a plastic Bus Stop sign.

iv.

She strokes my face, and says,
You look as young as the queen.

My father said, *No move is unplanned.*
Perhaps here, I have the upper hand.
I am not a queen, but a pawn

about to reach the other side.

Magpagpag

*a Filipino superstition: after you attend a wake, you need
to 'magpagpag' (go somewhere else to 'shake it off') before
heading home so that the spirit of the dead won't follow you.*

The mourners disperse.
All I hold now is the invitation
to your funeral. Dark liquor of lettering.
I am haunted by that smirk –

when I first met you, and you told me
that your name was spelled with an *i*
instead of *y*. And you were not
allergic to anything.

I drive to a resto for a bowl of miso.
I sip the cloudy broth and hear you,
humming *Take Me Home,*
Country Roads, your below-the-belt

jokes ruffling the hairs on my arms.
On my way home, the car behind honks
so loud the green light explodes
into a flock of parakeets. And I see you –

the day you did not want to shave,
crying that everyone had left, except Jack
Daniels. You said I was crap at my job
when I snatched the sanitary gel

you wanted to drink. Soundless rain
on the roof of my car. I am haunted
by your sober smile. I wash as if soap
was a scour, water whirls down

the drain. The rosy, whirlpool-mark
I left on the centre of your chest.
On my name pin, a homely
flake of your skin.

The Importance of Surgeons

Two men correct my mum and say they are
not gardeners but tree surgeons. She almost
changes to her nursing scrubs till the *keetweet*
of a long-tailed tit brings her down to earth.

The older man in mud-patched overalls
explains mere gardeners cannot determine
which limb to chop or at what height
a trunk should be sawn from the ground.

She asks what is the good of knowing
the depth or angle of a cut
for trees will not profusely bleed
or suffer hypovolemic shock.

At the breakfast table, she and I giggle
at how successful the operation is –
no infection acquired, she reports, holding
pieces of anchovy between her fingers.

Aren't people too keen on titles?
she throws the question to no one
in particular, looking out to the garden
where the sun shines correctly now.

Self-Portrait as Medicines

The sky at dawn is sodium valproate red,
like the gumamelas the little girl picks,
the petals she pounds with a rock.

The moon is a round tablet
of calcium carbonate, effervescent
on the forehead of a lake.

The coppices are shadows of strangers
you tread past in the symphony of rain,
or you stand with, on a tube to Farringdon.

The girl collects the flower's sap,
lathers it on her skin, make-believing
it is medicine. With a stolen match,

she boils bruised petals in a can.
The fire gnaws their garden,
and all night she kneels on mung beans;

arms widespread, balancing stacks
of books on her palms. The sky at dawn
is sodium valproate red. The moon

is effervescent on the forehead of a lake.
And the world is a small blue tablet
on the blackness of a tray.

If pulse is below sixty per minute,
Digoxin is omitted.
But there are harder things to count

than pulse rate; there are litres of tears,
there are mung beans. And days
she believed she could cure everything.

Dalampasigan

(Laiya, Batangas)

A great pawikan digs a hole
with its hind flippers, and buries the past
before returning to the ocean.

A certain memory disperses like steam
from an earthen pot. It doesn't leave
but only hides.

One day I will find it on the belly
of an upturned crab or in seaweed
that clings to a fishing net.

Perhaps it will find me the same way
salt settles on sunburnt skin
or in the shock of his black hair.

One night I will find the bahay kubo too,
the shy clinking of shell wind chimes.
I will sit on a table perfumed by the sea,

opposite a man who holds my memory
in the white grit on his philtrum.
And this time, I will forget

my snow-paralysed town, how good
a cherry stem-knotter I am
as I watch him swallow

a scad's scaly head, and take out
a sliver of bone
using only his tongue.

Aviva Dautch

Aviva Dautch teaches English Literature and Creative Writing at the British Library and works as a producer at Bethlem Museum of the Mind (the original Bedlam). She has an MA in creative and life writing from Goldsmiths and a PhD in poetry from Royal Holloway. Her poems are published in magazines including *Agenda, Modern Poetry in Translation, The North, The Rialto* and *The Poetry Review*. Aviva has been shortlisted for the Poetry Society's Geoffrey Dearmer Prize, was Poet in Residence at the Jewish Museum London from 2014-2016 and in 2017 received an award from the Hadassah-Brandeis Institute, Brandeis University for International Jewish Women in the Arts.

The House

Her mother barricaded her in behind household goods, newspapers, rotting vegetables, until the house became its own creature in the child's mind. How wave builds upon wave, a crowd roars to hear its own voice, worms halved multiply, and sound expands into silence. *Silence.* The way the piles of stuff swallowed her voice. The house was eating her: toenails thickening with fungus, red rings on her body expanding from pinpricks to a target. Books gave her temporary escape: books with tooth-marks, books with tears, crumbling spines, books burning – feeding the blaze the day the squirrels chewed through the electrical wires – books that had charted her way through the years blackened, covered with melted plastic, words disappearing before her eyes, going, gone. And then, nothing was quiet. The walls clattered as they settled into the earth. The bathtub she'd slept in sank gurgling into despair. The building retracted into itself. She – soft flesh – edged her way out. It's two years now. Two years since her mother buried herself past saving. There's no gravestone yet. Just clean grass, waiting.

Returning

Oh I could have stood for days in the doorway, positioned
between cracked wood and cracked wood, inert in my frame

like the pictures I'd scrutinised in white-painted galleries where
I used to spend afternoons, not for the art, but for the feeling

of empty space. Under my feet, the porch hummed with beetles –
shifting, my boot crunched a shattered carapace. It was a world

I hadn't entered for years, no human had, other than my mother,
my brilliant, desolate mother, small among her decaying hoard.

I could have stared and stared at the newspapers carpeting
a narrow path between the piles – their grimy print a Rorshach

collage – or at the tower of teetering bottles, all soda-shaped
but full of an indeterminate liquid, at the corsets and goggles

and red bills spilling awkwardly down the stairs. I was trying
to measure her madness by her cache. Futile! Stand still

long enough and everything degrades. The stench that pushed
against me, sweet with rot and mould, became the air I breathed

whose strangeness began to fade. This was home. Sunlight
warmed my back but in front of me the hall was clammy, cold.

The Emptying

After the fire I spoke to the house,
saying *I'm sorry* and *I'm leaving you.*
With each armful I took, charred and damp,
onto the lawn for sorting, I chanted

sorry, sorry, sorry but inside I was gleeful
this was the end. I saved financial records,
unopened envelopes with blackened edges
and corners chewed out, any photographs

whole enough to keep. What wasn't burnt
was infested so the rest went into the skip.
In protective clothing – shower cap, mask
and white babygro – I became a large child

stumbling around. The world shrank to piles
of salvage and a search for the necklace
with my Hebrew name Grandma brought home
on the last trip she made. Thirty-two tonnes

filtered, then taken to the dump, before I admitted
defeat. In Jerusalem my best friend found me
a new one, this time in silver, but when I wore it
I saw my golden name melting in the fire

or buried in decomposing refuse or wind-born
like the paper scraps that blew into the road
which my mother, raincoat buttoned over
her pink nightie, chased vainly down the street.

Mamaloshen

Mamaloshen (Yiddish) n. 'Mother-tongue'

Some accurate idea of language,
   its sinews and channels
and aromatic storage chests,
   was all I ever prayed for

when the world was rotting
   around her 'we're fine, we're fine' –
instead she matched kin
   with image, beyond with the wind.

Each time she knotted us together
   with lullabies
I dreamt of railroads
   and the ugliness of escape,

how words travel between
   countries like *kinder*
shedding unfashionable dresses
   and cadences of place,

mutating inside
   a cocoon of forgetting.
Their larvae bite holes in cloth:
   sudden remembered losses.

Habonim

*Ha'Bonim (heb): lit. 'The Builders'. 'Habonim' is
the name of an international Jewish youth group.*

The day the Wall fell we played the identity game –
had to run to a corner of the room depending
whether we felt British, Jewish, like British Jews
or Jewish Brits. On camp that winter we acted out

the journeys our grandparents made from Russia,
Poland, Lithuania, fleeing pogroms. The Holocaust
should have been next but perhaps they thought
we were too young. Instead, we became refugees

negotiating Checkpoint Charlie, winning points
for our team if we smuggled ourselves safely across.
Back at school in January, studying The Tudors,
I'd switch off, daydream, remembering how we built

the Berlin Wall with our bodies, one on top of the other,
rejoicing, limbs flying, when we came tumbling down.

Knots

That I didn't have to be *either/or* I didn't understand.
My favourite place, the green velvet settee – unraveling
its fringe slowly, twisting out the knots until each tassel
separated into component loops. My mother taught me

I was made from helixes and sequences, nucleotides
and codes. My father pulled me on his lap and told
the fable of a Rabbi who kept words in his pockets:
I am but dust and ashes. For my sake the world was created.

That was before, when black and white films made clear
who were the goodies and baddies, when I didn't know
how I'd spend years willing myself to bridge an ever-
widening split between fallible soul and failing body.

The Gathering

Bind him into the gathering of life
we pray in small voices when we are gathered
by this earthy hollow, locked by his death
into this gathering of people, sinking into a mud
that sweeps up over our toecaps and heels
staining the trousers we tuck into socks,
staining the skirts we gather up to our knees
and tendrils creep out of the ground and curl
around us, binding us to this grave this time
these words this man his absence
and we are yoked together by our hands
and we are yoked together by the plaintive song
we are calling into the wind, we are a litany,
we are beads rattling on a string, we string out psalms
into the wind, and it is morning –
there is an expanse of time until the sun will set,
an age has passed since the sun rose,
yet even now that we are walking away
it is morning – and as we raise our feet to take each step
the mud sucks us back in, we are pages sewn into a book
whose binding is fraying as we strain against it –
a book of prayers and psalms lit by the sun –
and the sun is shining, its rays are tentacles straining
to catch us, we are all gathered beneath the same sun
and as we fan out into the world we are gathered still.

DNA

Was I just your first quantifiable experiment? Motherhood,
our double helix of heredity,
a crucible of hope? You became more certain of your findings with
each teaspoon of serum and plasma,
your hold on reality loosening for a moment, making
your eyes dark with the consequences of your numbers
as you researched how to decode life.
This is what I remember, Mother: you (half mortal, half divine)
always working and nothing allowed to distract.
You didn't care about dinner or bedtime, reading
while I sat doing homework in the corner of your lab,
reading – scans, test-tubes, graphs – with a scientist's finesse,
so concentrated on the centrifuge spinning its vials of blood
you forgot how to speak to me.

You forgot how to speak to me,
so concentrated on the centrifuge spinning its vials of blood,
reading scans, test-tubes, graphs, with a scientist's finesse
while I sat doing homework in the corner of your lab.
You didn't care about dinner or bedtime reading,
always working and nothing allowed to distract.
This is what I remember, Mother, you – half mortal, half divine,
as you researched how to decode life,
your eyes dark with the consequences of your numbers,
your hold on reality loosening for a moment – making
each teaspoon of serum and plasma
a crucible of hope. You became more certain of your findings with
our double helix of heredity.
Was I just your first quantifiable experiment: motherhood?

The Bottle Lid

Hoarders seem to process information in unusual ways, e.g.
categorizing possessions by shape or size, rather than by use.
  – Professor Randy Frost, 'Compulsive Hoarding and Acquiring'

It's metal with fluted edges, the kind of cap
you find on a bottle of beer or old-style cola,

which in its own way is strange: she hated fizz,
advocaat with a bleeding heart of cherry brandy

was more to her taste and then only on festivals.
It lies in a plant pot, alongside the inner-tube

of a toilet roll, handfuls of coins, a kosher salami
rancid in its plastic skin, Great Aunt Bertha's

eternity ring. But this isn't a random collection –
like playschool, today we're heading through

the round window. In my mind, the lid becomes
a porthole, an expanding pupil. In hers, it's valuable,

worth more than me, tense as a coiled spring.
As a child I'd watch her work, sketching family trees

to track trails of genetic disease. Shading signified
illness then death, dots meant carriers uninfected

themselves. Carefully she drew squares for the men,
empty circles to represent healthy, female lives.

What She Kept

My baby photos, school reports, The Famous Five and Winnie-The-Pooh. Gray's Anatomy in three separate editions. The Manchester Evening News, Jewish Chronicle, Jewish Telegraph and Jewish Gazette. Adverts and leaflets, tokens for money-off. Cardboard boxes and plastic bags. Seedlings in yoghurt pots. Fluffy toys bought for her great-nephew and nieces, rejected and now infested with fleas. Food on every surface, all kosher but past the sell-by-date. Duplicates of everything. A broken photocopier in the hall no one could reach to fix. Bandages and sterile strips, burn-bins full of used needles and bloodied cotton wool. In the glass-fronted bookcase: Bibles and candlesticks, wine glasses and Holocaust memoirs, a bottle of nail-varnish remover separated into layers of sediment and oil. Hundreds of melted lipsticks, shading from magenta to red. Never-been-worn cardigans and dresses hanging from doorframes and banisters, laid out like people on each of the beds.

Shame

And so I intervened: clear-eyed, competent,
  muscling my way past her objections
and pleas for time. Silent too long as a child,
  this was my chance to inflict my will

on her hoard: peeling bin bags from the roll
  with elation, the swing of my hips
under each load carried from the house
  cocky as a honky-tonk jive.

I'm doing this for her as well as me,
  I told myself, as armfuls of her clothes
settled at the bottom of the skip,
  proud of my decisiveness, of knowing

how to assess what was truly worth saving
  from the heaps of the torn and rusted,
the rat-chewed and the hard-worn. Through
  all those days of being polluted

by the stink, of gloves and antiseptic
  and piles 'for sorting' crushing
her carefully maintained garden,
  through black ribbons of unspooled

videos catching at my hands and feet,
  through mildew and foetid sheets,
through the salvaging of bills
  and bank-statements into plastic folders

laid out alphabetically on the lawn,
  through the fortnight staying
with her brother, who tried – although
  not that hard – to hide his resentment,

through conversations
      with neighbours and police
and social services, through careful budgeting
      and renting a flat, I was fast and ferocious.

It wasn't until there was nothing
      left to do that I noticed how small
she was: shriveled like the snail bereft
      of its shell and caught by the salt-trap

my well-meaning mother had set on the path
      a few days before to protect
the sweet-peas in their neat borders,
      advertising the beauty of their home.

Tahara

Tahara (heb.): lit. 'purification'; the process
of ritually preparing a body for a Jewish burial.

On the table, carnations.
I hate them. These furled, crimped pinks
my mother would buy.
Even now
she is tightly wound –

the women twist the sheet around her,
over her face,
before letting me into the room,
give me dirt from the Holy Land
to sprinkle into her plywood coffin,

read the Hebrew prayer with me
in their shtetl accent.
I slow them down,
too tired to translate sense
as well as sound.

We lift the lid together, nail it closed.
It's a good deed to care for a body,
to accompany a soul to its grave.
It takes time to learn how to wash
each fold of skin,

how to fold a shroud.
They had studied for this.
They had taken their time.
Longer than promised, than usual.
I'd waited with a friend –

we were meant to recite psalms,
instead we stared
at the linoleum,
could only imagine
what they worked to cleanse.

Clearance

I was desperate to free myself
from the lingering smell
of her, from my fear

she'd crumpled her loss of me
into balled-up tissues
tossed under the bed

where they gathered blue dust
and spider webs,
were shredded into the nest

where a mouse
bedded down her babies
and nurtured them

but when the men threw
her mattress into the skip
and dismantled the frame,

I found a floorboard
rotted down, collapsing
into itself with a fretwork

of splinters and, rolled into the trough,
a bottle of anti-ageing serum
without its cap.

After I rubbed it on my trousers
the cracked glass shone
like amethyst, its fractures

an intaglio engraving
of the very wrinkles
it promised to eradicate.

I scooped out a little cream
and, despite myself,
smoothed it into my skin.

Yeridah

*Yeridah (heb f. noun): lit. 'descent' – used to describe someone
who was born in Israel but moves to the diaspora*

The only prayer you ever said was the Traveller's Prayer
for the start of a journey: *May it be your will Eternal One,
Lord our God and God of our ancestors that we reach
our desired destination.* The days lengthened as you paced
the rooms of our upside down flat, its kitchen attic-high
with a view falling from rooftops to the still, black canal
where Hasidim strolled the towpath in their heavy coats.
Young enough to have nothing to do but idle away hours
with a slowly cooked meal, I brewed tea from mint leaves,
watched you washing up the Israeli way, under a torrent
of running water. I loved the space we made in the heart
of London's Jewish ghetto, a photograph of your land
above the bed where you tore my Englishness from me
then slipped through my fingers to your next almost-home.

Ghazal

after Agha Shahid Ali

Beloved, I fear the language of shame is Hebrew.
Once loss was all, now loss is hard to frame in Hebrew.

Yours is the well from which my sorrow springs,
your water, but the earth that steals the rain is Hebrew.

With you I have railed at the shuttered sky
and wept, yet know that tears are not the same in Hebrew.

In the wilderness Jews yearned for a home –
the home that we built, the home that we maim, is Hebrew.

Uprooting olive trees, scarring the soil,
we fight, crush foes like fruit, apportion blame in Hebrew.

Each body-bomb blown up and rocket fired
inscribes my anger when the land aflame is Hebrew.

Like the smear of dust on skin, grief mars me.
We brush off dust but who can brush off pain in Hebrew?

Don't protest we're not our brothers' keepers:
the tale that poets wear the mark of Cain is Hebrew!

Witness our songs – *I am yours Beloved*
and you are mine – witness Solomon's claim in Hebrew.

To resist complicity, 'not in my name!' –
how? when the root of my soul, of my name, is Hebrew.

The Foundry

Weathered as the house
which went to ruin

and took my childhood
by the throat,

I would lift a head
that wasn't mine

from the table and cast it
in plaster, pour liquid

bronze into the mould,
hollowing it out

to decrease the weight.
This is what I called

patination: weeks
of chemicals and heat

stripping away layers
for the praise of strangers.

There was always
the possibility of harm

but my art came easily,
bleaching the shadows

I exhaled
with each long breath.

Sarala Estruch

Sarala Estruch is a London-based writer, poet and critic. She holds degrees in English Literature and Creative Writing from Goldsmiths College and Birkbeck College, University of London. Her poetry, fiction, creative non-fiction and reviews have appeared or are forthcoming in *Wasafiri, The North,* and *The White Review,* among others. Her work has been commended for the Wasafiri New Writing Prize and the PBS National Student Poetry Competition. In 2017, Sarala was selected for the Ledbury Emerging Poetry Critics initiative, a mentorship programme designed to redress the diversity imbalance in UK poetry reviewing culture.

England: A Love Story, or The English Dream

London, 1978

do you remember / love / that day at the student hostel on Cross Street / the way the light tilted in / at the window to settle / on two émigrés / as we waited for our keys / except now we'd arrived / we were émigrés no longer but immigrants / carrying a larger suitcase of connotations / me pale-skinned in 70s flares / European features and freshly bobbed hair / you brown-skinned in new polished oxfords / and your unequivocal Indian nose / that day the sunlight illuminated us equally / and we thought nothing of *difference* / only of *novelty* / we were in love / with a country gleaned / from school textbooks and the photographs / your mother kept in the album of her childhood / gardens with rosebushes and hedgerows / cherry-cheeked men and women chirping *good morning* / from behind the garden gate / neighbourly / it was not neighbourly / the way they looked at you / when you stepped onto a bus / or the names you were christened / at the restaurant where you worked / in the kitchen / suds up to biceps / hands deep / in the crud of this country / washing and washing / fingers still aching the next morning / as you took notes in law school / while back in the country of your birth / you dined with nabobs / had already received a bachelor's degree / these days as we walk arm-in-arm down London streets / turning our eyes and ears inside-out / to deflect the stares and the curses / *(Paki! Wog-lover!)* / I recall the school textbooks / manicured lawns fences and gates / cherry-cheeked persons with neighbourly faces / and think *yes* / *the English are neighbourly* / *as long as you stay* / *on your side of their gate*

Kesh

When one too many crane-necked
buttoned-up Englishwomen crosses
to the opposite pavement, when he
grows tired of the mutterings that
trail him like the British clouds,
when the job interviews become
predictable and his landlord raises
the rent on his damp-infested flat
for the second time in six months

he sharpens his blade, approaches
the mirror above the sink, the stink
of bleach and mildew rioting
in his nostrils, making his eyes smart
as he unravels the skeins of navy-
blue cotton, cloth falling away
from his head as if from the body
of a woman to reveal the black
glistening ocean beneath.

As he lifts his hand, closes his fist
around the rope, he tries not to think
of Biji or her fingers washing,
combing, plaiting in the evenings
of his childhood or his father
who taught him, on the dawn of man-
hood, how to knot a patka and tie
a pagh so that if ever a person
were in trouble they would see
the turban and know to approach
not turn their head in repulsion
as they did here in London in 1973.

A prayer is lost somewhere between
tongue and teeth as he pulls the strands
taut as the strings of a sitar and brings
down the blade back and forth, back
and forth, witnesses the cold silver cut –

Kesh: (from Punjabi keś): The uncut hair and beard worn
as one of the five Ks (the distinguishing signs of the Sikh
Khalsa) by Sikh men. The wearing of the turban or pagh
(pronounced 'pugg') is considered an extension of kesh.

They Came for Us in the Night

for Mildred and Richard Loving

They came for us in the night
as we were sleeping in our bed.
The crash of the front door going down
the flashlight wounding our eyes.

All was white
panic scuttled in our hearts like roaches.
Then out of the whiteness, a voice:
Who's the woman you're sleeping with, Sir?

The brightness passed, replaced by shadow.
And there was the Sherriff, ruling the shadow,
so close we could see the sweat smothering
his brow. I clung to my husband then –

strong arms, firm torso. His whole body
was screaming though lips remained closed
so I spoke: *I'm his wife.* But I could already
feel the hands prising me off

and the metal cuffs, cold as nothing
I'd ever touched. The Sherriff hoisted me
to my feet. Leant in close, breathed hot
in my ear: *Not here, you're not.*

Dreaming of Love in Uttar Pradesh

i.

It's the first thing anyone says when she tells them
she is dating a Sikh: *You're not expecting him*
to marry you, are you? The Sikhs are clan-like,
zealous in their blood-ties – this is well known.
But he has shown her passages in the Guru Granth Sahib
upholding the sanctity of love over caste and creed,
has told her marriage is the union of two souls
and souls are casteless, creedless. But are they
raceless? The question on the cliff of her tongue
as she follows his eyes, his lips, the elasticity
of his cheeks, not the words on the page, wanting
to believe and almost believing him.

> *ii.*
>
> *I pass a mirror in our rented flat*
> *and see myself – unlikely bride*
> *of you. Slight-framed, moon-*
> *skinned, not Indian let alone Sikh;*
> *Spanish-Italian-Algerian-French*
> *descendant of wanderers, migrant workers:*
> *sailors, mechanics, seamstresses, cleaners.*
> *And your father's brother is the CEO*
> *of the Bank of India, and your cousin*
> *married a Maharaja.*

iii.

He takes her to the family home in Uttar Pradesh –
adobe palace with a rooftop prayer room made of glass.
On the porch, waiting, are his mother and father
who smile, shake her hand and tell her *Welcome*.
But their eyes and voices are not smiling.

iv.
Waking in this foreign bed
with the wind running outside
as if it is being chased
and you in another bed
in another room
on the other side
of this ancestral kingdom,
I am a spring
beneath a skin of soil
a touch away from breaking
through.

v.
My mother-to-be approaches the window, hesitates
before the curtain, her heart like a river.
She finds lashings of rain, the sky clouded over
and strangely bright. The trees tremble.
She thinks of my father, a familiar stranger
since she arrived in this country, and the faraway look
his family wear whenever she enters a room
as though they are already watching her leave.
The storm enters her, the brisk wind pushes her
up against the glass of herself and she knows
she should have listened.

vi.
Our love was a kingdom
they refused to let us enter.

Cracked Pavement

That November day, I recall

were more cracked than usual

from concrete slab

without touching a blemished square

We had traversed Dynevor Road

and Edward's Lane

on a fissured square

even hopped and accidentally

on a concrete skeleton

muttered under my breath

I'd lost a life, had only one left

I noticed the park gates

My mother had begun to talk.

in the walk. There was no one

only the chestnut trees

My mother began to speak

the paving stones

making my game of leaping

to concrete slab

a treacherous one.

the length of Church Street

and I had already stepped

a tilted slab

landed single-footed

of a paving stone

Rest in peace.

was close to quitting when

were seven jumps ahead.

We had reached a break

around

half-naked branches.

and all at once I knew

this was the purpose of the walk

the park at all but anywhere

and held in the air

for the listener to receive

There was something

(the vocal cords resisting

together for support)

Her face a broken paving stone

a single word.

... why your father didn't come ...

... a heart attack

Then the consonants and vowels

and stomped their feet

jumped up and down

and the pavement collapsed

my mother and I, down

when they swear they don't want

but they aren't yet willing

the destination had never been

words could be uttered

long enough

their weight.

about her voice

pressing themselves

that made me look up.

and on it was scrawled

She was saying

and

in the middle of the night ...

dropped to the ground

on the paving stones

the concrete smashed

and we sank

to the place where people go

to give up on the living

to give up on the dead.

Blame

He died
of blood starvation, red and white
cells blocked from swimming
to the heart by arteries clogged
like drains in autumn.

It was all that meat, my mother
said. *It was the cigarettes.*

I knew he loved me more than
anyone because he had told me.
If I had told him to quit smoking
and go vegetarian, his arteries
would have been clean estuaries
waiting to carry passengers home.

Such is the vision of a seven-year-old –
believing herself to be the sun
around which the universe turns,
knowing herself to be a god: omnipotent
and thus responsible.

My Indian grandmother

isn't Indian.
She turns up at my mother's flat
        five weeks after my father's death,
majestic with silver curls
        like a taller version of the Queen.
Call me Gran. I struggle to greet her.
        My father never mentioned her
or any family member. My mother
        shakes her hand with poise
while, in the kitchen, the kettle screams.

My Indian grandmother takes me
        shopping for the day. *You can choose*
anything you like. By the dress rack
        she has a million questions.
She wants to know my favourite everything
        at the Pick N Mix aisle.
I fill the paper bag, at her insistence,
        with pear drops and marshmallow twists,
don't tell her I'm not interested in things
        as I used to be: that liquorice,
for instance, doesn't taste as sweet
        and red and green have lost
their radiance.

In the back of the taxi, her head turned
        absorbing London streets
I get a closer look – regal neck
        and silver locks, pale skin
gently creped. It's strange to think
        my father's hair will never grow white,
that his skin won't soften and fold
        into itself like a rose that holds
onto its stalk long after having passed
        its peak.

The Measure of Water

What is agony of the spirit?
To advance toward death without seizing
hold of the Water of Life

– Rumi, 'Love is the Water of Life'

Because my mother won't let me go to Indonesia
to lose myself in relief work in the aftermath
of the tsunami, I wind up here – Jamaica,
March 2005 – being driven along the stretch
of the peninsula from Port Royal to Kingston
by Didi, a nun in orange robes, having finally
succumbed to a yearning for a sense
of belonging that is more fluid than concrete.

It is sunset, the water on either side of the road
turning scarlet as we drive toward an imposing
rise she tells me is Blue Mountain, the island's
highest peak. When the road widens, Didi veers
left, away from the mountain; we are no longer
surrounded by sea but by buildings already
too shrouded in shadow to be properly seen.
By the time she points at a road and says
Down there's the school where you'll be working
it is already deep-sea dark and the street trails off.

She warns me not to dress in red or green
on the days I work because the island is divided
into two main gangs and Mountain View
is the horizon where sun and sea converge.
We are often forced to close the school.
The shock of simple words throwing me back
to the peninsula, no – further, into the water
and I am once again a swimmer in a rip tide.

The conversation shifts to global warming.
She says Port Royal was once the trading capital
of the New World, home to pirates
and desperados till an earthquake shook the city
and a tsunami followed, sucking buccaneers
and bricks into the belly of the sea. Now Jamaica's
coastlines are eroding and rising water levels
threaten to claim what remains.

At the spiritual centre, Didi shows me my room:
a yellow-walled rectangle with metal slats
in the windows in place of glass and two yoga mats
draped with a clean sheet for a bed.
I rest my backpack in the closet and follow her
downstairs where she has prepared a dinner
of vegetable stew, seasoned with ginger
and coconut milk. Its simplicity makes sense.

Later, she will teach me to meditate, to breathe
in through the nostrils and imagine my body
is like the sea at sunset, slowly filling with light
especially the points of my spine and the chakras
between my eyes and at the crown of my head.
She teaches me a mantra to repeat over and over
till it drowns out all stray thoughts and leaves me
clean as a stone submerged.

Something Like Purgatory

In my grandparents' bedroom in their second home
on the outskirts of Delhi, the oceanic roar of heavy traffic
racing in through the meshed windows along with the blood-
red rays of the setting sun, my grandmother is dreaming.

She lies beneath two or three thick *razai*
woven with a single flower pattern repeated compulsively
like waves on the ocean or the way our bodies breath:
in and out, in and out. Her body, under the blankets,

is a trickle of water evaporating, and there is nothing
she nor I can do to stop it. She jokes
about how the stomach cancer has made her high-fashion
material, says *Vogue* will headhunt her now.

Of course this is all happening decades too late.
She is eighty-one years old. The only things her stomach
will accept: a square or two of her favourite Cadbury's,
the rainbow of pills she swallows daily. She wants to please,

tries the homeopathic remedies my mother has sent.
Keeps saying how much better a woman my mother was
to my father than my father's eventual wife.
I wonder what she dreams of now: her childhood in Bristol

or the day she met my grandfather – a young, turbaned man
with a sanguine smile. Perhaps she is dreaming of the day
my father was born. In her dream, she can still hold him,
his chest rising and falling against hers.

I hope she does not dream of his death.
When she wakes, she will tell me forbidding my parent's marriage
is the biggest regret of her life. It is also mine, though I don't say it.
When she asks for forgiveness, I will give it.

Red Delhi

(i.m. Enid Nat)

Grandma was sick
so I packed my red coat,
boarded the plane
and took a direct route

(London-Delhi
with no stop-offs).

I prayed that I would make it,
get there before the wolf –
knowing he is versed
in shortcuts, in entering

and breaking
people's lives.

But when I arrive
he is already there,
propped up
in my grandmother's bed.

There – in the fingers
clawing the bedcovers

the silver tail trailing
like tears down her spine.
There – in the hollows
of her cheeks

sunken mines of gone skin
but most of all

he is in her eyes –
bulbous balls
protruding from sockets,
startled and wandering, lost.

If only this were a fairytale,
the woodcutter would be outside.

He would enter with his axe raised
and carve the wolf clean out.
But I am no surgeon,
my tools are paper and pen

and so I write this poem
to remember the woman

my grandmother was:
strong-boned, long-necked,
possessor of all her flesh,
her heart like a song

that continued to play
long after she was gone.

Consequences of Not Knowing
My Father Tongue

after Kayo Chingonyi's 'Kumukanda'

Since my parents did not circle the Guru Granth Sahib
as holy men sing songs of union with God, did not
receive semolina sweets or the blessings of my father's
relatives, I do not know how to drape a sari or make tea
the Indian way; I speak English and French but no Punjabi
or Hindi, forever confusing my *Chachas* with my *Chachis*
and hoping for understanding when I switch to *Uncle*
and *Auntie* instead. And when, at my uncle and aunt's
engagement, I stand beside my uncle – acting in my father's
place as keeper of rings – I bless this engagement, bless
this new beginning, knowing love carries more weight
than the human tongue.

Chacha – father's younger brother (Punjabi)
Chachi – father's younger brother's wife (Punjabi)

To the Wounded Among Us

after Ada Limón

But everyone is wounded a little.
What are hearts but purple, pumping
wounds? What are we but hearts
travelling in skin suits?

Today we are tired of listening.
This morning we woke with our ears full
cochleae still reverberating with gunshot
and the bombs we detonated yesterday

in yet another failed attempt to colonise
each other. And when, over breakfast,
you gifted me your tall barricade of a back
I bit into my toast to occupy my throat.

Did you ever consider love as a kind
of deafness? Not only the act of making love
when the tympanic membranes are so pumped
with blood we can hear nothing

but the sound of ourselves pulsating;
but love itself, the way it can refuse
to read words on lips – preferring to hear:
bend of arm, incline of neck, susurration

of skin. The way love can translate
an argument *(I hate you, I'm leaving)*
into the clamour of blood pouring through veins
screaming *I love you. I'm hurting. Hold me.*

Thoughts While Kissing

Still, after all we've traveled
      – years, countries, continents –
         you still taste the same
as that first time: midnight, Blue Mountain peak
      moonlight rushing
         through the fingers of trees.

When Bolt lost (his final race)

clouds paused in the sky

rain froze into ice

the wind held her breath

and rivers raced upstream

in a frenzied attempt

to reverse the clock

even the globe forgot

to turn on its axis

just long enough

for the world to be lost –

or so it felt to me

who had to deliver the news

to my five-year-old son

that the fastest man alive

had lost a race

that the fastest man of all time

had not won first place

that the world's eighth wonder

(a Jamaican, like his father)

was only human after all

and I'm sorry son, I'm sorry

but we've so much

to be thankful for

we've so much

to be proud of

because, in truth, he did not lose

he was unplaced

and even the greats

fall sometimes

but they always get back up.

ACKNOWLEDGEMENTS AND THANKS

Romalyn Ante:
'The Making of a Smuggler' was commended in Battered Moons Poetry Competition 2017.
'Antiemetic for Homesickness' was published in Manchester Poetry Prize 2017 (joint-winner).
'Way Back Home' won the Creative Future Literary Award, 2017.

Romalyn Ante is grateful to Pascale Petit for her advice and support.

Aviva Dautch:
'Tahara' was first published in *The North* Issue 50 and will be anthologised in *Poems about Britain* (The Emma Press: 2018).
'Ghazal' was first published in *Modern Poetry in Translation* 3/11 and anthologised in *Her wings of glass: ambitious poems by contemporary women poets* (Second Light: 2014).
Audio recordings of 'The House', 'Habonim', 'Tahara' and 'Ghazal' feature in the British Library's *Between Two Worlds: Poetry and Translation* collection.

Aviva Dautch is grateful to Jo Shapcott and Mimi Khalvati for their guidance and encouragement.

Sarala Estruch:
'Kesh' and 'England: a Love Story, or the English Dream' were both longlisted in the 2017 National Poetry Competition.
The epigraph of 'The Measure of Water' is taken from Jelalludin Rumi's poem 'Love is the Water of Life' from *Teachings of Rumi: The Masnavi* (translated by E.H. Whinfield) (Octagon Press, 1994).
'Consequences of Not Knowing My Father Tongue', after Kayo Chingonyi's poem 'Kumukanda' from *Kumukanda* (Chatto

and Windus, 2017). This poem was previously published on MIROnline.

'To the Wounded Among Us', after Ada Limón's poem 'To the Busted Among Us' from *sharks in the rivers* (Milkweed Editions, 2010). The title and opening line of this poem are variants on the title and opening line of Limón's poem. 'To the Wounded Among Us' was previously published on CAMPUS, The Poetry School online platform.

Sarala would like to generously thank Martina Evans, Jacob Sam-La Rose, Lesley Sharpe, Sandeep Parmar and Daljit Nagra for their help and encouragement.